P9-APD-437

LEXINGTON AND CONCORD

DAVID KING

Twenty-First Century Books

A Division of Henry Holt and Company

New York

Twenty-First Century Books
A Division of Henry Holt and Company, Inc.
115 West 18th Street
New York, New York 10011

Henry Holt® and colophon are registered trademarks of Henry Holt and
Company, Inc.
Publishers since 1866

Published in Canada by Fitzhenry & Whiteside Ltd.
195 Allstate Parkway, Markham, Ontario L3R 4T8

Printed in the United States of America on acid free paper ∞.

Created and produced in association with Blackbirch Graphics, Inc.

Picture Credits
Cover and pages 4, 7, 9, 12, 15, 16, 18, 19, 20, 21, 22, 28, 30, 31, 35, 37, 40, 43:
North Wind Pictures; page 45: Library of Congress Collection; pages 46, 48,
49, 50, 51, 53, 54, 55: © 1995 Kelly/Mooney.
All maps by Bob Italiano/© Blackbirch Press, Inc.

Library of Congress Cataloging-in-Publication Data

King, David C.
    Lexington and Concord / David C. King
        p.   cm. — (Battlefields across America)
    Includes bibliographical references and index.
    Summary: Presents an account of a critical turning point in U.S. history, the
battles that plunged the thirteen colonies into war with Great Britain, a war
known as the American Revolution.
    ISBN 0-8050-5225-9
    1. Lexington, Battle of, 1775—Juvenile literature. 2. Concord, Battle of,
1775—Juvenile literature. [1. Lexington, Battle of, 1775. 2. Concord, Battle of,
1775. 3. United States—History—Revolution, 1775-1783—Campaigns] I. Title.
II. Series
E241.L6K525 1997
973.3'31—dc21   97-29420
                                                                                                        CIP
                                                                                                        AC

CONTENTS

P A R T   O N E

THE ROAD TO REBELLION

In the year 1763, the people of both Great Britain and the 13 American colonies joined in celebrating a great triumph. With help from the colonists, the British had just won a long and costly war with France, a victory that forced the French to give up all their possessions in North America. Great Britain now ruled the world's greatest empire, and the American colonists were proud to be part of it.

ince the first struggling settlements had been established in James-
town, Virginia, and in Plymouth, Massachusetts, in the early 1600s, the
colonies had grown and prospered under British rule. By 1763, more
than 1.5 million people lived in towns and farm villages along the
Atlantic Coast and were steadily pushing inland toward the West.
Although the colonists had come from many different lands, they considered themselves to be subjects of Great Britain.

This loyalty toward Great Britain and the British monarch, King
George III, however, did not last.

The Colonists React to British Actions

King George III and his ministers in the British Parliament had decided
that since the 13 colonies had benefited from Britain's victory over
France, the colonists should share in the cost of maintaining Britain's
newly enlarged empire.

The king and Parliament decided to tighten their control over the
colonies and to generate some additional tax revenue. To accomplish
this, the British government passed a series of measures, one of which
provided for the creation of writs of assistance—general warrants that
allowed British officials to search homes and businesses for smuggled
goods and to try accused smugglers before a British judge rather than in
a colonial court.

< 5 >

< 6 >

To raise money for Britain, Parliament passed a tax law in 1765 called the Stamp Act. This new law required the use of special paper for all printed materials. The paper was imprinted with an official stamp showing that the new tax had been paid. Newspapers, documents, advertisements, and even playing cards were included in this tax.

And in order to maintain peace with the Native American tribes on the North American frontier, in 1763 the king issued a proclamation that essentially forbade colonial settlements beyond the crest of the Appalachian Mountains. The British government also sent 10,000 soldiers to the colonies to defend the empire. The colonists were required to provide barracks and supplies for the troops.

These actions touched off a storm of protest from the colonists—a reaction that the British government had not expected. The American colonists felt that denying them access to lands in the West was unfair. They had fought and died for those lands in Britain's war with France, and they felt they had earned the right to expand their settlements westward. The colonists also questioned the need for a British army of 10,000 soldiers during peacetime, and they resented the writs of assistance. The protestors argued that one of the most cherished rights of British citizens was the right to a trial by a jury of one's peers. This right was now being violated.

A Storm Over Stamps

More than any other measure, however, it was the Stamp Act that most angered the colonists. Although it was not a heavy tax and had been used many times before in Britain, the Americans objected to the *way* it was being imposed. In the past, any measure to raise revenue in the colonies had come from their own colonial assemblies.

Colonists joined together to protest unfair British policies.

Now, for the first time, Parliament was taxing the colonists directly even though they had no elected representatives in Parliament.

Throughout the colonies, outraged colonists who called themselves "patriots," began organizing opposition to the Stamp Act. They formed groups named the Sons of Liberty and the Daughters of Liberty and rallied to encourage people to boycott (refuse to purchase) British goods. Some patriots wrote eloquent pamphlets and newspaper articles that argued that there should be "no taxation without representation" in Parliament. Many colonists also protested in the streets, burning the government's stamped paper and bullying stamp officials. Within three months, all of the king's tax collectors in the colonies had resigned.

< 8 >

Many patriots also felt that it was time for the colonies to unite in their actions against the British policies. A special Stamp Act Congress was called and delegates from 9 of the 13 colonies met in New York in the fall of 1765. The delegates passed a petition asking that the Stamp Act be repealed (withdrawn). The petition was then sent to the British government.

The colonists' protests brought mixed results. Trade with British merchants dropped dramatically as a result of the boycotts and, in the spring of 1766, Parliament voted to repeal the Stamp Act. At the same time, however, Parliament also passed the Declaratory Act, which insisted on Britain's complete power over the colonies "in all cases whatsoever."

Crisis and Calm

In 1767, a year after repealing the Stamp Act, the British government again tried to tax the colonists. This time, a series of taxes called the Townshend Acts were placed on goods being imported into the colonies. The finance minister, Charles Townshend, reasoned that since the colonists had never protested such import duties, or taxes, before, he had simply increased them to raise revenue. He also set up a Customs Board to enforce payment of these duties.

Once again, the British failed to foresee how strongly the colonists would react. And once again, the colonists organized boycotts of British goods and wrote pamphlets in opposition to the taxes.

While these protests were taking place, an ugly incident occurred in the Massachusetts colony involving British troops. It led to the first bloodshed in the quarrel between the colonists and the British government. In late 1768, two regiments of British troops had arrived in Boston. During the months that followed, the people of Boston became increasingly annoyed by the presence of

Angry colonists set fire to the British customs ship, the Gaspee.

the red-uniformed soldiers, whom they called "lobster backs" or "redcoats." On March 5, 1770, a gang of men and boys began jeering at a group of British guards and pelting them with snowballs. Tempers flared out of control, and the soldiers opened fire, killing five colonists.

The more radical patriots, led by Samuel Adams, were always looking for ways to stir up anti-British feeling. They labeled this tragic incident "the Boston Massacre," and it soon became a symbol of British tyranny. As one patriot wrote, the Boston Massacre "fed the fire of liberty and kept it burning with an incessant flame."[1]

< 10 >

The relationship between the colonies and Great Britain then entered a period of calm. The violence on the streets of Boston had shocked people on both sides of the conflict. The new British prime minister, Lord North, repealed the Townshend Acts. To make certain that the Americans recognized Parliament's authority, however, he kept the tax on imported tea.

Although the next three years were relatively calm, minor incidents occurred that kept the Sons and Daughters of Liberty active. In June 1772, a British customs ship, the *Gaspee*—used to enforce British tax laws on goods being shipped to the colonies—ran aground off the Rhode Island coast while in pursuit of smugglers. That night, nine boatloads of patriots, disguised as Native Americans, boarded the ship, forced the crew off, and set the *Gaspee* ablaze. Outraged by this act of rebellion, the British government sent a commission to investigate the incident, although no suspects were ever identified.

At about the same time, Adams persuaded the people of Boston to establish a Committee of Correspondence. This committee would inform the patriots in other colonies of events in Boston that involved British violations of colonists' rights. Within a few months, each colony had formed its own correspondence committee. These groups became a valuable way for patriots everywhere to exchange information and ideas.

Tea: The Fuse on the Powder Keg

In May, 1773, the British Parliament once again misjudged the mood in the colonies when it passed a seemingly harmless measure called the Tea Act. This new law was intended to help the financially troubled British East India Company by giving it a monopoly (exclusive control) on all tea sold in the colonies. The patriots were outraged by this measure. They argued that, if the British could control the

< 11 >

tea trade, what would prevent them from controlling all business in the colonies?

When shiploads of tea began arriving in late 1773, patriots in every colony were ready. In some ports, they simply locked the tea in warehouses. In others, they forced the ships to turn back without unloading the goods. The patriots of Boston, however, organized a more dramatic form of protest. On the night of December 16, a band of colonists, loosely disguised as Indian warriors, boarded the ships and dumped 342 chests of tea into the dark waters of Boston Harbor.

The patriots were delighted by this "Boston Tea Party." John Adams, a leading patriot, wrote, "The die is cast....This is the grandest event which has ever yet happened since the controversy with the British opened."[2]

King George III and Parliament were outraged by the tea protest. In the early months of 1774, the furious king and his ministers guided a series of measures through Parliament that were intended to punish Bostonians and the colonists of Massachusetts—the port of Boston was ordered closed until the colonists paid for the destroyed tea. This cut off the city's vital trade entrance. Many provisions in the charter of Massachusetts were suspended, severely limiting the colony's self-government. In addition, a new Quartering Act required all colonists to open their homes to British soldiers if barracks were not available. In a separate measure, known as the Quebec Act, the boundary with Canada was moved south to the Ohio River, thereby cancelling the claims of several colonies to the lands west of the river. To enforce these "Coercive Acts," as they were called, a British general named Thomas Gage was sent to Boston to become its governor. The British government also sent more warships and troops to the colonies.

The king and Lord North were convinced that the Coercive Acts would put an end to the colonial protests. "The die is now cast," the

In December 1773, colonists dumped hundreds of chests of tea into Boston Harbor.

king wrote, his words echoing the phrase used by John Adams, "the Colonies must either submit or triumph."[3] The king was determined that they would submit.

Instead of feeling coerced, however, the colonists were angered as never before by what they called the "Intolerable Acts." Reactions to these acts occurred throughout the colonies. In Virginia, the elected assembly protested the new laws as a violation of the colonists' basic rights. When the royal governor—an official appointed by the king—ordered the assembly dissolved, the members met illegally at Raleigh Tavern in Williamsburg. They passed a resolution stating that "an attack made on one of our sister colonies, to compel submission to arbitrary taxes, is an attack made on all British America."[4] Wagonloads of supplies were sent to Boston from every colony. George Washington, already well known for his youthful leadership in Britain's war with France, echoed the feelings of many when he wrote, "Shall we, after this, whine and cry for relief, when we have already tried it in vain?"[5]

< 13 >

Patriots like Washington wanted to take a stronger stand than in the past. The British measures, far from forcing the colonies to submit, had created something the British never thought possible— a powerful new feeling of unity among all 13 colonies. In September, 1774, a total of 55 delegates from the colonies met in Philadelphia for the First Continental Congress. The Congress was the first political body to represent the 13 colonies.

The Congress drew up a list of resolutions, demanding the repeal of the Intolerable Acts and denouncing Britain's taxation of the colonies. The delegates formed a Continental Association, which called for a complete boycott of all trade with Great Britain. Unlike earlier boycotts, however, this one would be enforced—the names of all violators would be published and their merchandise would be seized. The delegates agreed to meet again the following May if their demands were not met.

At the same time, the patriots in Massachusetts were preparing to fight the British, if necessary. They began organizing each town's militia into groups of "minutemen"—special units that would be ready to take up arms at a moment's notice. They also formed a Provincial Congress, which began meeting in the town of Concord, Massachusetts.

As the winter of 1774-1775 approached, the time for compromise was running out. A few members of Parliament urged the king and his ministers to remove the troops from Boston and repeal the hated Coercive Acts. One member declared, "You may spread fire, sword, and desolation, but that will not be government....No people can be made to submit to a form of government they say they will not receive."[6]

But King George III and his ministers were not about to give in to the colonists' demands. In November 1774, the king wrote to Lord North: "The New England governments are in a state of

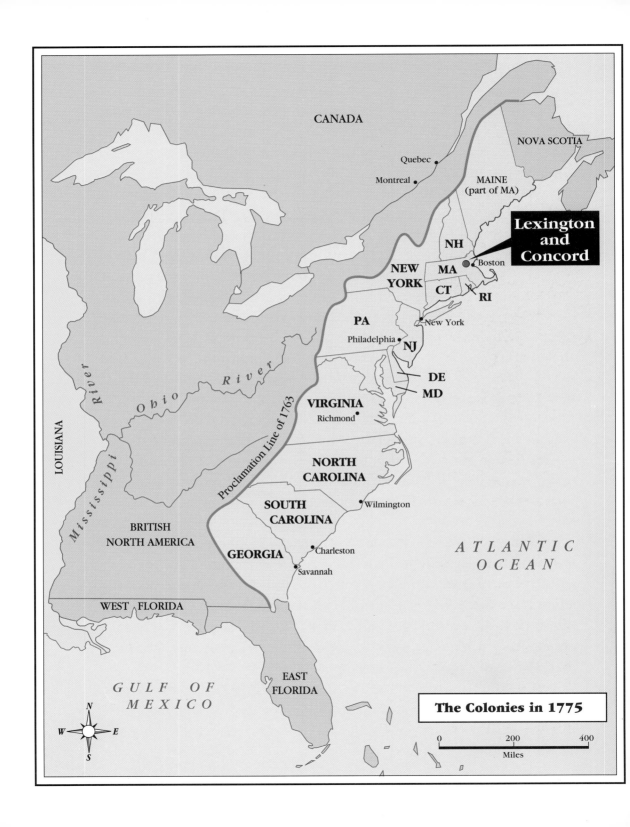

CANADA

NOVA SCOTIA

Quebec

Montreal

MAINE
(part of MA)

Lexington
and
Concord

NH

NEW
YORK

MA

Boston

CT

RI

PA

New York

Philadelphia

NJ

DE

MD

VIRGINIA

Richmond

Proclamation Line of 1763

NORTH
CAROLINA

SOUTH
CAROLINA

Wilmington

BRITISH
NORTH AMERICA

GEORGIA

Charleston

Savannah

*ATLANTIC
OCEAN*

LOUISIANA

Mississippi River

Ohio River

WEST FLORIDA

EAST
FLORIDA

*GULF OF
MEXICO*

N
W E
S

The Colonies in 1775

0   200   400

Miles

Patriots made their own weapons and prepared to defend their rights.

rebellion; blows must decide whether they are to be subject to this country or independent."[7]

Even the most enthusiastic patriots, however, were not thinking of independence. They believed they were merely demanding their rights as British citizens. As Boston patriot Dr. Joseph Warren wrote in February 1775, "It is not yet too late to [settle] the dispute amicably. But...if once General Gage should lead his troops into the country [to enforce the Coercive Acts], Great Britain may take her leave of all America."[8] The fuse that had been lit by the Boston Tea Party was now burning rapidly.

P A R T   T W O

LEXINGTON AND CONCORD:
THE OPENING SHOTS OF THE AMERICAN REVOLUTION

By the spring of 1775, the British government had grown impatient with General Gage. The king and the Parliament wanted Gage to march inland from Boston and force the "rebels" to obey the provisions of the Coercive Acts.

Gage, however, was not confident that this assignment was possible. Although Boston Harbor was crowded with British warships, Gage had only 4,000 troops at his command and controlled only the city of Boston. Gage had plenty of spies in the countryside—colonists called Tories, or Loyalists, who were deeply opposed to the patriot cause. From the Tories' reports, Gage knew that the militia in every town were storing up munitions (weapons) and were preparing to fight. In a letter to his superiors, Gage explained that, "while the colonials are not held in high estimation by the troops, yet they are numerous and are worked up to a fury."[1] The general asked for 20,000 more soldiers, but his request was denied.

On April 14, 1775, Gage received a stern letter from his superiors, ordering him to take immediate action against the rebels. Reluctantly, Gage organized a force of 700 of his best soldiers and ordered them to destroy the militia's munitions that were stored in Concord, Massachusetts.

Gage knew that if his mission was to succeed, complete secrecy was essential. If the patriots learned that a column of British troops was on the march, the entire countryside would take up arms. Gage told his plans to his top officers, including the column's commanders, Lieutenant Colonel Francis Smith and Major John Pitcairn. The soldiers themselves were not informed of their destination.

Thomas Gage

By 1775, British General Thomas Gage had spent 19 years in North America, most of the time as commander-in-chief of the British forces in the colonies. After being named governor of Massachusetts in 1774, and while still commander-in-chief of the army, Gage became increasingly obsessed with the idea of secrecy. He was convinced that there was a spy among his closest associates, who informed the patriots of his every move. There is some evidence that this spy was actually Gage's wife Margaret. She was an American and was related to Philip Schuyler, one of the leading patriots in the colony of New York. (Ironically, Schuyler was later accused by patriots of spying for the British.)

The king of England and his ministers did not approve of Gage's handling of the situation in Boston. He was called back to Britain in late 1775, and never again attained a prominent military position. Although there is no evidence that Gage suspected his wife of betraying him to the patriots, the couple separated when they returned to Britain and were never reconciled.

The Road to the Edge of War

The patriots, meanwhile, were keeping an eye on every move the British made in Boston. One of those who kept watch was Paul Revere, a well-known silversmith and engraver. "Toward the spring [of 1775]," Revere recalled, "we frequently took turns, two and two,

< 19 >

to watch the soldiers by patrolling the streets all night."[2] Revere also helped to establish an elaborate warning system to alert the towns around Boston if the British marched inland.

Gage was well aware that his movements were being watched. To prevent the patriots from spreading the alarm, he sent advance patrols into the countryside on the night of April 18. The patrols were supposed to stop any messengers riding toward Lexington and Concord. The patriots did not know exactly where the British patrols were, but they expected that the British might intercept any messengers heading for those two towns.

As the British troops began gathering that night, Revere and his companions sprang into action. Revere had arranged for a signal to be sent from the steeple of Boston's Old North Church: Two lanterns would be shown if the British moved by water across the Back Bay to Charlestown; if they took the longer route by land, a single lantern would be the signal.

An hour before midnight, when Revere was certain of the British route, he ordered the two-lantern signal flashed from the steeple. He was then rowed across the Back Bay to the Charlestown shore. A group of patriots, having seen the two lanterns, were

Lanterns in the Old North Church tower were used to alert the patriots that the British were on the move.

John Hancock was Boston's wealthiest merchant, building much of his fortune by smuggling goods past British customs inspectors. He was an early leader of the patriots and was head of the Massachusetts Provincial Congress. After the battles of Lexington and Concord, he became president of the Second Continental Congress and was the first to sign the Declaration of Independence. He wrote his signature in bold strokes, he said, so that "the king can read it without his spectacles." Late in the war, he became the first American governor of the state of Massachusetts.

John Hancock

Paul Revere was one of colonial America's best known craftsmen, both as a silversmith and an engraver (one who cuts, or engraves, letters or pictures into copper plates that are used for printing). Revere was one of the earliest leaders of the patriot cause, serving as an organizer, courier (messenger), and propagandist (promoter of a cause). His engraving of

waiting for Revere on the other side with a swift horse. Revere immediately set off on his historic 18-mile ride to alert the militiamen in Lexington and Concord. Another messenger, Billy Dawes, had already started for Lexington and Concord by another route.

In later years, a legend grew around Revere's "midnight ride," indicating that he alone had alerted every militia along his journey. In fact, dozens of other riders were involved. As each town was the Boston Massacre was printed throughout the colonies. It became a major piece of patriot propaganda, showing the British soldiers firing on the unarmed colonists at point-blank range.

During the American Revolution, Revere manufactured gunpowder for the patriot armies and served as an engraver for the Continental Congress. His brief experience as a militia commander ended badly, and he went back to making gunpowder. After the war, Revere returned to his work as a silversmith and engraver. His silverware and pewterware are considered outstanding examples of American craftsmanship.

Revere also developed a method to prevent the hulls of wooden ships from rotting—the hulls were coated with sheets of copper. One of the first ships to receive this treatment was the *USS Constitution,* which later became famous as "Old Ironsides." After the Revolutionary War, Revere continued to dress in the clothing of a militiaman until his death in 1818.

Paul Revere

alerted, the local militia leader immediately sent one or more riders to warn other towns. Signal guns, fires, and church bells were also used to sound the alarm. In this way, news of the British column's movements spread through the countryside with amazing speed.

By the time the British column came ashore in Cambridge, their mission was no longer a secret. As they began marching down the road to Lexington, a British soldier recalled, "the people had

Paul Revere, as well as other brave messengers, spread the warning that the British were approaching.

begun to fire their alarm guns and light their beacons to raise the country."[3]

After escaping a British patrol, Revere arrived in Lexington around midnight, where he delivered his warning, and waited for Dawes. When Dawes arrived, the two men set off together for Concord along with a young doctor named Samuel Prescott. They were stopped almost immediately by one of Gage's patrols. As they

PAUL REVERE'S RIDE: THE LEGEND

In the years following the Revolution, Paul Revere was remembered both for his work as a craftsman and for his contributions to American independence. During Revere's lifetime, his ride to Lexington on the night of April 18, 1775, was not considered especially memorable. He was only one of several messengers who had spread the alarm on horseback.

In 1861, nearly a century after the battles of Lexington and Concord, Henry Wadsworth Longfellow, one of the nation's most beloved poets, wrote a poem entitled "Paul Revere's Ride." It begins with the famous lines, "Listen, my children, and you shall hear/Of the midnight ride of Paul Revere."

Longfellow's poem soon became widely popular and transformed Revere's ride into legend. The poet depicts Revere as a lone messenger, riding through the countryside to warn the patriots of the approaching redcoats. More than 100 years after the poem was first published, it was still being reprinted. It was memorized by schoolchildren and read aloud on patriotic holidays.

In the 1960s, historians began pointing out that the poem was a romantic distortion of fact. Longfellow had written, for example, that "It was two by the village clock/ When he came to the bridge in Concord town." As we now know, however, Revere never made it to Concord that night. The most important objection raised by historians is that the poem obscures the fact that the countryside was alerted by means of an elaborate system of messengers, signal guns, and church bells. While Paul Revere played a key role that April night, he was not quite the solitary courier depicted by the poet.

Despite the scholars' criticism, the poem continues to be popular. Its haunting images and easy rhythm make it enjoyable both to read and to hear. The poem also highlights the dedication and courage of an individual who participated in one of the most historic events in American history.

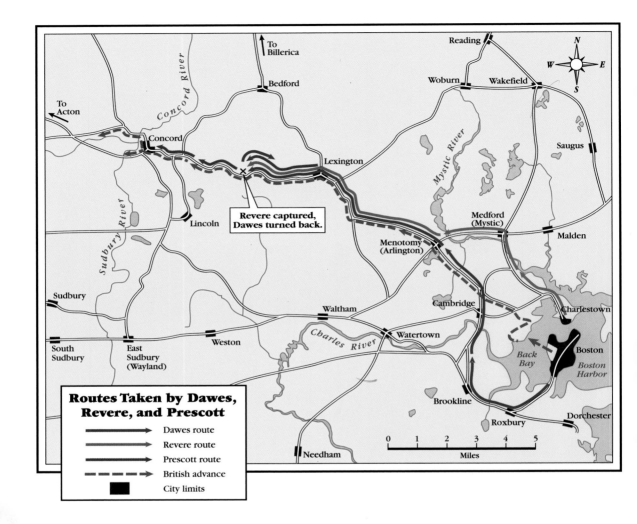

Routes Taken by Dawes, Revere, and Prescott

- ⟶ Dawes route
- ⟶ Revere route
- ⟶ Prescott route
- ⟶ British advance
- ▬ City limits

Revere captured, Dawes turned back.

were being questioned by the British officers, the three patriots, still on horseback, managed to break free of their captors. Prescott and Dawes escaped. Revere, however, rode into a patch of woods and was recaptured by another group of British soldiers. (By this time, Dawes had had enough excitement for one night and he made his way back to Lexington. Prescott resumed his journey to Concord.) Meanwhile, increasingly alarmed at the sound of the signal guns, the redcoats released Revere, but kept his horse. They rushed back

< 25 >

toward Boston to meet the main British column. Revere made his way back to Lexington on foot.

By this time, minutemen from a dozen towns were gathering at pre-arranged points called mustering places, mostly at officers' homes, or taverns. About 70 men under the command of Captain John Parker met near Lexington Green. At first there was confusion about what was happening and about whether or not British troops were really marching toward their town. Just before dawn, a rider arrived with the news that the column was approaching Lexington.

The stage was now set. For the first time in colonial history, Americans were ready to use their weapons against British soldiers—men they had always thought of as their fellow countrymen.

Lexington: The First Clash of Arms

Captain Parker ordered his men to form two lines at the north end of Lexington Green. At dawn, six advance companies of redcoats under Major Pitcairn marched into view. As the British approached, Parker is reported to have told his men, "Don't shoot unless fired upon. But if they mean to have a war, let it begin here!"[4]

Parker, however, then saw that his men were hopelessly outnumbered, and ordered the minutemen to disperse. As they started to leave, still holding their weapons, someone fired a musket—no one ever knew which side the shot came from. Both sides accused each other of firing the first shot. According to the Americans, one of the British officers advanced on horseback, raised his sword, and shouted, "Lay down your arms, you damned rebels, or you are all dead men!"[5] The front line of redcoats immediately fired on the minutemen. "While the company was dispersing and leaping over a stone wall," said a minuteman named Sylvanus Wood, "the second platoon of the British fired, and killed some of our men."[6]

THE ILL-FATED COMMANDERS AT LEXINGTON

When they faced each other on Lexington Green, neither John Parker, captain of the patriot militia, nor the British commander, Major John Pitcairn, had much longer to live. Pitcairn would die in battle, and Parker would succumb to disease.

John Parker lived his entire life in Lexington, working as a farmer and a part-time mechanic. A supporter of the patriot cause, he was elected captain of the town militia. In April 1775, although he was seriously ill with tuberculosis, he insisted on fighting at Lexington. Parker died from the illness in September of that year. His famous statement, "...If they mean to have a war, let it begin here!" is engraved on a stone monument on the Lexington Green.

Major John Pitcairn was commander of General Gage's regiment of marines. Although few marines marched with the British column, Pitcairn was sent to Lexington and Concord because he was the senior major in the British command, and he was respected by the patriots for his sense of fairness and decency. Gage thought that if negotiations were needed, the Americans would listen to this man. A New England minister had described him as "a good man in a bad cause." Two months after the battles of Lexington and Concord, Pitcairn was shot and killed at the battle of Bunker Hill. The man who shot him was the African-American minuteman Salem Prince, another veteran of the April 19 battle.

The British officers seemed to lose control of their men, who fired wildly at the retreating Americans. Some of the minutemen stopped and fired back. "We took aim at the main body of the British troops," Corporal John Monroe reported, "the smoke preventing our seeing anything but the heads of some of their [officers'] horses, and discharged our pieces....I saw Jonas Parker [a relative of Captain Parker] struggling on the ground, with his gun in his hand,

< 27 >

apparently attempting to load it...the British came up, run him through with the bayonet, and killed him on the spot....The [British] regulars kept up a fire, in all directions, as long as they could see a man of our company."[7]

Another minuteman, Jonathan Harrington, was wounded but managed to stumble and crawl about 300 feet across the road before dying in front of his horrified young wife and son. When the thick smoke of battle drifted from the green, eight minutemen lay dead and ten had been wounded. Only one redcoat had been wounded.

With fife and drum music playing, Smith's companies then joined Pitcairn's, and the full column began marching toward Concord, six miles to the west. The battle of Lexington was over. Although it was not a major battle, the conflict at Lexington would

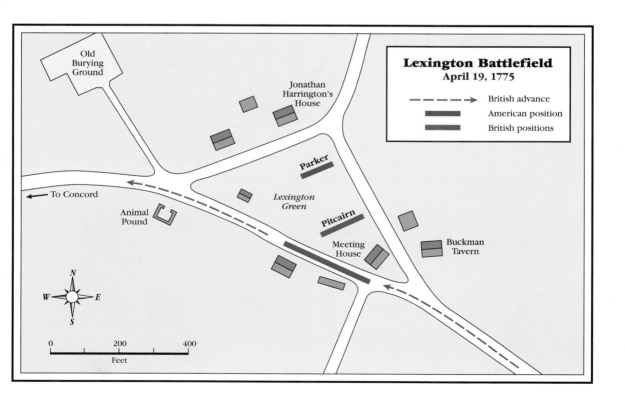

A painter and an engraver created this scene from the battle of Lexington after hearing accounts of the event from militiamen.

have a powerful impact on the course of history. As the stunned residents of Lexington watched the victorious British troops march away, the minutemen faced an important decision: Should they return to their homes and submit to British rule, or should they stand firm and fight back? Later that afternoon, the men followed Parker across the fields to Concord.

< 29 >

The Battle of Concord: "The Shot Heard Round the World"

As the British column marched the six miles from Lexington to Concord, the peal of church bells and the sound of signal gunfire continued to draw militia units from miles around. Samuel Prescott had already arrived in Concord, giving the patriots plenty of time to remove and hide the munitions—many of which were stored at the home and mill of Colonel James Barrett. Some of the weapons were buried in freshly plowed farm fields where they could be dug up later. During this frenzied work, a minuteman galloped into town with news of the Lexington battle.

A group of about 150 Americans marched from Concord to meet the British. Seeing the long line of redcoats from a hill, their steel bayonets glistening in the morning sun, the militiamen retreated to Concord. Fifes and drums on both sides were playing—as minuteman Amos Barrett put it, "We had grand music."[8]

Knowing that they were outnumbered by the British, the militia leaders decided against trying to defend the town. Instead, they moved their men, now numbering about 250, to Punkatasset Hill, just north of Concord. Colonel Barrett took command and, like Captain Parker at Lexington, although he was willing to fight, he wanted to make sure that the British fired first.

The British troops marched into Concord and took control without firing a shot. Lieutenant Colonel Smith sent one detachment of redcoats to destroy the munitions at Colonel Barrett's house. A second detachment stood guard at the North Bridge. The other British troops began searching the buildings of Concord. They set fire to several gun carriages—two-wheeled wooden platforms used for moving cannons—and the fire spread to the town hall. Much of Concord might have gone up in flames had it not been for the

The minutemen on Punkatasset Hill watched the smoke from Concord's burning buildings.

courage of a widow named Martha Moulton. Risking her life, Moulton found the British commander and insisted that he order his men to put out the fire. Although threatened by several officers, Moulton repeated her request until Smith finally ordered that the flames be doused.

The Americans on Punkatasset Hill were infuriated at the sight of smoke rising from the village. Barrett ordered his men to move closer to the North Bridge, but still cautioned them not to shoot first.

At the bridge, British Captain Walter Laurie, with only 96 men, watched the Americans, now numbering 450, advance. He and the other British officers were amazed to see the militiamen marching in perfect battle order. Laurie sent a messenger to Smith, "begging that he would send more troops."[9] He then withdrew his men to the east

< 31 >

side of the bridge and formed three companies, one behind the other. With this arrangement the first company would fire, and then move to the rear to reload. The second company would then come forward to fire. Laurie ordered some of his men to tear up the planks of the bridge—but they were too late.

On the west side of the bridge, the Americans hesitated for a moment. Captain Isaac Davis, from nearby Acton, raised his sword and shouted, "I haven't a man who's afraid to go.... March!"[10]

With Davis and his 38 men in the lead, the militiamen advanced again. The nervous redcoats, without waiting for an order, opened

American militia advance on British troops at North Bridge in Concord.

< 32 >

fire. Their shots were followed quickly by those of the second company. Two Americans, including Davis, were killed instantly, and two others were wounded. The militiamen immediately shot back, killing three British soldiers and wounding several others. Then, as the astonished patriots stared in disbelief, the redcoats suddenly turned and ran, scrambling back to the main column in Concord.

This brief encounter at the North Bridge was memorialized a half-century later in a poem by Ralph Waldo Emerson as "the shot heard round the world."[11] Emerson was not exaggerating. The Americans had done something of enormous consequence—they had shot and killed soldiers of the king. The colonists of Massachusetts were now officially at war with Great Britain.

At the time, the patriots seemed dazed by what had happened and unsure of their next move. One young minuteman rushed across

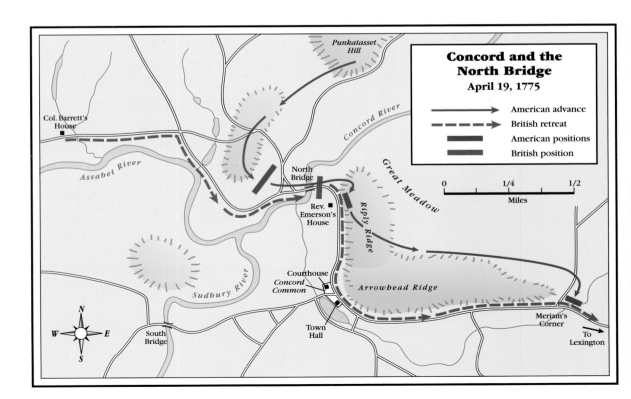

< 33 >

the bridge and brought his hatchet down on the head of a wounded redcoat. This horrible act would have serious consequences throughout the day. When the British troops saw their mutilated comrade, they condemned the Americans as butchers and swore to take revenge.

After seizing the North Bridge, about 200 militiamen positioned themselves behind a stone wall. They watched as the full British column marched toward them. "If we had fired then," minuteman Amos Barrett said, "I believe we could have killed almost every officer there was in front; but we had no orders to fire."[12] The redcoats, however, changed direction to avoid a full-scale battle. Smith and Pitcairn, the British commanders, tried to figure out their next move.

Battle Road

Although no one knew it then, the day's real battle had not yet begun. It was now almost noon, and the British seemed uncertain of their route back to Boston. They could see that the surrounding hills were now swarming with American militiamen—at least 2,000 of them. The only possible means of escape was down the narrow, 18-mile road by which they had come 12 hours earlier.

At noon, Lieutenant Colonel Smith finally had the British column moving. For nearly an hour, the countryside was eerily quiet, except for the rhythmic sound of marching soldiers. About one mile east of Concord, the column crossed a little bridge at Meriam's Corner, and there some of the British fired shots into a house.

As if those shots were a signal, musket fire began hitting the British column from all directions. The Americans shot at the British soldiers from behind stone walls, trees, houses, and barns, and then ducked for cover before running ahead to fire more shots. "All the hills on each side of us were covered with rebels," a British officer

< 34 >

reported, "so that they kept the road always lined and a very hot fire on us without intermission."[13]   To protect the main column, Smith put small units of men called flanking companies on both sides. These soldiers fired back steadily at the Americans.

Some of the heaviest fighting took place along the road at two sharp bends that became known as the "Bloody Angle."   As the British column slowed to round the two turns, militia units opened fire from both sides of the road.   Militiaman Edmund Foster recalled that "the enemy was now completely between two lines of fire. They ordered out a flank guard on the left to dislodge the Americans from their posts behind large trees, but they only became a better mark to be shot at."[14]

As the British neared Lexington, the redcoats were approaching a state of panic. "Our ammunition began to fail," British Ensign Henry De Berniere recalled, "and the light companies were so fatigued with flanking, they were scarce able to act."[15]   The growing number of wounded added to the confusion. "We began to run rather than re-treat in order," De Berniere continued. "The whole behaved with amazing bravery but little order."[16]

The British trooops staggered back to Lexington Green, where they expected to be defeated in one final assault. Suddenly, some of the exhausted soldiers let out a cheer. On the outskirts of town, they could see hundreds of redcoats—a relief column sent by Gage. The general in command of the relief force, Lord Hugh Percy, had already organized the 1,000 men in battle formation. He also had two small field cannons that were immediately put into action.

The first shots from Percy's cannon threw the American militia-men into confusion and halted their advance. Smith's men took advantage of this lull to retaliate for the endless sniper fire they had endured. They burned three houses and looted many others in Lexington. William Gordon, a patriot minister, said that "many

The redcoats came under heavy fire as they retreated from Concord toward Lexington.

houses were plundered of everything valuable that could be taken away, and what could not be carried off was destroyed."[17]

Even with Percy's relief force, the British still faced a harrowing 12-mile march to safety. As Percy prepared to march at about 3:00 in the afternoon, a new American commander, General William Heath, took command of the scattered militia units. Moving rapidly between the companies, Heath organized flanking units to keep the British under almost constant fire. Whenever the British column passed a militia unit, the men of that unit would withdraw and head for a

< 36 >

position further down the road. Lord Percy wrote later that his troops were "under incessant fire, which like a moving circle surrounded and followed us wherever we went until we arrived at Charlestown."[18]

The town of Menotomy, about halfway between Lexington and Charlestown, was the scene of some of the day's bloodiest fighting. As one British soldier wrote, the redcoats "were so enraged at suffering from an unseen enemy that they forced open many of the houses from which the fire proceeded, and put to death all those found in them."[19] (Most of the women and children had been moved to safety while the British were marching toward the town.) At Cooper's Tavern, Rachel Cooper and her husband managed to escape but, she reported, two elderly customers "were most barbarously and inhumanely murdered, being stabbed through in many places, their heads mauled, and their skulls broke."[20] Reports of British brutality and of the battles spread through the colonies and convinced many Americans that the British were a savage enemy. Twenty-five Americans and at least forty British soldiers were killed at Menotomy.

The running battle continued through the afternoon until well after sundown. The British finally reached the hills of Charlestown, where they came within the protective range of the British warships in Boston Harbor. The Americans wisely decided to halt the attack, and the battle-weary redcoats were ferried back to Boston during the night.

The day-long battles of Lexington and Concord had finally ended. The British had suffered heavy casualties—73 dead, 174 wounded, and 26 missing; the American losses were less than half the British total—49 dead, 39 wounded, and 5 missing.

Considering the unconventional nature of the fighting, it is a credit to the courage of the redcoats and the leadership of their officers that their losses were not far greater. Over a period of about 20

THE BRITISH COMMANDERS

Lieutenant Colonel Francis Smith, the commander of the British column, was a cautious, slow-moving officer who never displayed great leadership abilities, but who always managed to gain the approval of his superiors. General Gage had chosen Smith to lead the march to Concord because he was the senior officer in the unit.

The men serving under Smith, however, were often frustrated by his plodding leadership. At the North Bridge in Concord, for example, when Captain Laurie sent an urgent message requesting help, Smith was slow to respond. As British Lieutenant John Barker recalled, Smith ordered two or three companies to aid Laurie, "but put himself at the head, by which means he [prevented] 'em from being time enough, for being a very fat heavy man he would not have reached the bridge in half an hour, though it was not half a mile to it."[21]

After news of the British losses at Lexington and Concord reached Britain, some people thought that Smith should be removed from his command. But the king and his ministers continued to favor Smith, who served throughout the war, and even rose to the rank of general.

Thirty-two-year-old **Lord Hugh Percy**, Gage's second in command, was one of the most respected officers in the British army. He was also one of the wealthiest men in Britain. Although Percy felt his government's policies toward the colonies were an enormous mistake, he had little respect for the Americans he met in Boston. "The people here talk much and do little," he wrote in a letter home.[22] His leadership helped to save the British from an even greater disaster on April 19, and the event gave him a new respect for the courage and fighting ability of the patriots. After two more years of warfare, Percy resigned his commission and returned home.

Lord Hugh Percy

< 38 >

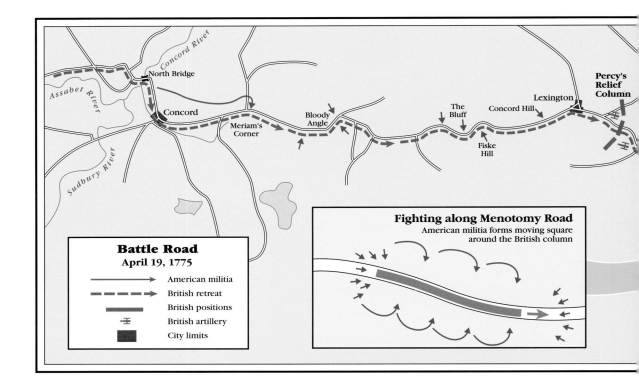

hours, they had marched almost 40 miles. During the second half of that journey, the redcoats came under constant attack from a well-protected enemy.

For the Americans, the day was a stirring military victory as well as a great boost to their morale. The patriots had more than held their own against the king's best soldiers. They had fought primarily in the method that they preferred, using natural barriers and buildings for protection, and avoiding a head-on confrontation with a massed army. The British were unprepared for this manner of fighting and weren't able to effectively retaliate. The Americans had learned to fight this way from the Indians, and it would serve them well in the years ahead.

< 39 >

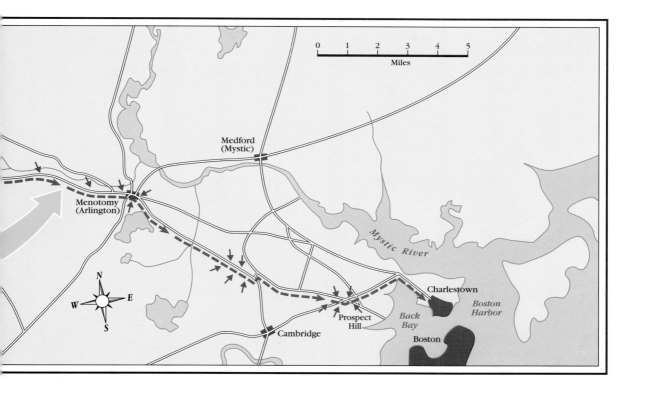

The Outcome: The American Revolution

"The shot heard round the world" was one of history's critical turning points. The battles of Lexington and Concord would plunge the 13 colonies into a full-scale war with Great Britain. This war lasted six years and became known as the American Revolution, or the War for Independence.

In the spring of 1775, several weeks passed before people realized the full importance of what had happened. The militiamen and their officers who had been harassing the British column on April 19 did not go home when the day's fighting ended. Instead, one company after another set up camp on the hills around Boston. New

William Heath was a gentleman farmer with no military experience before the battle of Concord. As a leading patriot, however, he had become convinced that the colonists would be forced to fight for their liberty. He thought that skirmish warfare would be the best way for them to fight. Skirmish warfare is when troops fight from protected positions, such as behind a tree or stone fence, rather than facing a massed army in an open space.

For several years, Heath read countless books on this subject. Many of the patriot militiamen had learned about skirmish warfare from the Native Americans. Heath introduced a new element, however, to their method of fighting. He organized groups of men into flanking units that moved in a square formation on either side of the enemies' troops.

William Heath

units continued to pour in from the neighboring colonies. Soon there were 16,000 patriots forming a solid half-circle around the city, and trapping the British against the harbor.

No one was sure what would happen next, but it was clear to both the British and the Americans that the battles of Lexington and Concord had changed the course of their future. The colonists of Massachusetts were now at war with Great Britain. How would the other colonies respond?

Heath tried to help organize the many militia units engaged in the running battle from Lexington to Charlestown but, by his own admission, his main activity was cheering the troops on. Heath was later made a general and served under George Washington. Early in 1777, however, during the battle for New York, Heath badly mismanaged an attack on a British stronghold. Washington never again allowed Heath to command troops in battle.

Samuel Whittemore may have been the best patriot marksman on April 19, 1775. The American militiamen in general had dreadfully poor aim that day. Most patriots were farmers, tradesmen, and craftsmen, rather than trained soldiers. Of the estimated 75,000 shots fired by the patriots throughout the day's fighting, only 247 hit enemy soldiers— 299 out of every 300 shots missed their targets!

Samuel Whittemore had no trouble with his aim. Although he was 78 years old and crippled, accounts tell of Whittemore firing so rapidly and with such accuracy that British troops were sent to dislodge him. The elderly patriot supposedly killed one more redcoat with his musket and wounded two others with his pistol before he was shot in the face at close range and bayoneted 13 times. After the battle, Whittemore was still alive and was taken to the home of a doctor. Whittemore recovered and lived to the age of 96.

Even with express riders (messengers on horseback) and swift sailing schooners, it took more than two weeks for reports of the battles to reach all the other colonies. During that time, some patriot leaders expressed their doubts. "There's no knowing where our calamities will end,"[23] wrote John Adams the day after the battles. When the news reached Virginia, Thomas Jefferson wrote, "This accident has cut off our last hopes of reconciliation, and a frenzy of revenge seems to have seized all ranks of people."[24]

< 42 >

To many patriots, however, war seemed to be inevitable. They were convinced that the time had come for all the colonies to unite against the British. On March 23, 1775, a full four weeks before the Lexington and Concord battles, patriot Patrick Henry had delivered a fiery speech before the Virginia Convention. "We must fight!" Henry had declared. "The war is actually begun! The next gale that sweeps from the north will bring to our ears the clash of resounding arms!" (The "clash of resounding arms" referred to the likelihood of battles such as Lexington and Concord.) Henry concluded his speech with the famous challenge, "Is life so dear or peace so sweet as to be purchased at the price of chains and slavery? Forbid it, Almighty God—I know not what course others may take; but as for me—give me liberty, or give me death!"[25] The patriots of Virginia were thus ready to fight even before news of the battles arrived.

Even moderate patriots were ready for action. George Washington, like Henry, felt that Americans must choose either to fight or to be enslaved. "Unhappy it is," he wrote of the battles, "to reflect that a brother's sword has been sheathed in a brother's breast, and that the once happy and peaceful plains of America are either to be drenched in blood or inhabited by slaves. Sad alternative! But can a virtuous man hesitate in his choice?"[26]

The British, too, realized that the patriots in all the colonies were now likely to commit themselves to war. "You may depend on it," Lord Percy wrote, "that as the rebels have now had time to prepare, they are determined to go through with it...."[27] He also warned that the fighting skills of the patriots were not to be taken lightly. "Whoever looks upon them as an irregular mob will be much mistaken," he declared. "They have men among them who know very well what they are about...and this country, being much covered with wood and hilly, is very advantageous for their method of fighting."[28]

Patrick Henry delivered his famous "Give me liberty, or give me death!" speech before the Virginia Convention in March 1775.

< 44 >

Reports of the Lexington and Concord battles continued to spread through the colonies and across the Atlantic to Britain. Meanwhile, the Massachusetts Provincial Congress, which was first established in 1774, met again and voted to raise an army of 30,000 militia troops. The delegates sent written requests to the other New England colonies, asking for additional troops.

The Second Continental Congress met in Philadelphia on May 10, 1775, to find a way to conduct a war that was already in progress. Among the delegates were some of America's leading figures, including George Washington, Thomas Jefferson, Patrick Henry, Benjamin Franklin, and both John and Samuel Adams. But this great gathering did not constitute a government. The war would have to be fought with whatever cooperation the Congress could achieve among the 13 colonies.

Despite the difficulties, the delegates had no intention of withdrawing from the war that began at Lexington and Concord. With John Hancock as president of the Congress, they voted to create a Continental Army from the militia camped outside Boston. Washington was the unanimous choice for commander-in-chief.

The American patriots still faced a number of momentous decisions. For one thing, they had to decide their reason for fighting. Few Americans were thinking of independence from British rule, and most felt that they were simply fighting for their rights. Even General Washington remained loyal to King George III. At Washington's camp near Boston, he began each evening meal with a toast to the king. A full year of fighting would pass before the Americans were ready to break all ties with Britain, and to declare their nation's independence.

In 1776, after the Declaration of Independence was issued, the Americans still needed to win their independence by fighting a war against the world's greatest army and navy. Three factors were

The Declaration of Independence was ratified by the Continental Congress on July 4, 1776.

crucial to America's victory: (1) the willingness of enough people to support a bitter and difficult six-year war; (2) although Washington lost more battles than he won, he always managed to keep a Continental Army in the field; and (3) a brilliant American victory at the battle of Saratoga in 1777 convinced France to recognize American independence and to enter the war as their ally. Finally, with one last victory at Yorktown in 1781, the struggle for independence was won, ending the dramatic confrontation that began when 70 minutemen faced British troops on Lexington Green.

PART THREE

HISTORY REMEMBERED

Probably no other battle in America covered more ground than the running battle that began at Lexington, moved to Concord, and then extended 18 miles back to Charlestown. Major highways now cross some of the former farmland and meadows where the fighting took place. Electronics plants cast shadows over parts of Battle Road. Despite these intrusions, however, key battle sites and buildings have been preserved and serve as living reminders of the day that launched America's War for Independence.

America's battlefield sites provide a unique record of some of the most dramatic events in our nation's history. No book or television program can quite match the extraordinary feeling a visitor gets at one of these sites. At Concord's North Bridge, for example, one can imagine the tension and anxiety of America's citizen soldiers as they faced troops from the world's mightiest army across the narrow bridge. A visit to battlefield sites is not only an exciting way to learn about history, but is also a way to honor the courage and dedication of those who fought to create and preserve our democratic nation.

Despite their historical importance, the preservation of these battlefield sites shouldn't be taken for granted. Modern society often encroaches on the land of one battleground or another, to build shopping malls or housing developments. Government budget cutting has also threatened some of these landmarks. Several sites were closed to visitors from 1993 to 1994 because no funds were available for staffing.

It is important that all Americans join in the ongoing effort to preserve our historical legacy—not only for today's visitors, but for future generations as well.

< 47 >

< 48 >

Minuteman National Historical Park

The National Park Service, an agency of the U.S. government, manages the Minuteman National Historical Park, which consists of three different units—two in Concord and one in Lexington.

A good way for visitors to begin a tour of these sites is to walk along Battle Road, just to the west of Route 128. This is part of the park's Battle Road Unit, which also includes a Visitor Center where exhibits, an excellent film, and a sound-and-light program are presented. Following a map provided at the Visitor Center, visitors can walk the four-mile stretch of Battle Road from Fiske Hill just outside Lexington, to Meriam's Corner, one mile east of Concord. The sound of traffic recedes as the road bends around the "Bloody Angle," and pedestrians will understand the trapped feeling the British must have experienced as militiamen fired at them from both sides. As a recent visitor commented, "Walking that piece of the Battle Road is like stepping back in time more than 200 years."

The park covers 750 acres and the National Park Service is continually restoring and relocating buildings of the period, striving to recreate as much of the colonial setting as possible.

Battle Road remains much as it was at the time of the battle of Lexington.

Two of the park's units are located in Concord. The Wayside Unit includes the home of Samuel Whitney, Concord's muster officer, which shows visitors the traditional furnishings of a patriot family's house. Just outside the old village center is the North Bridge Unit. Here, too, visitors can feel history closing in around them. More than one million people visit this spot every year, walking along the soft gravel path past the Old Manse (the home of Reverend William Emerson, grandfather of writer and scholar Ralph Waldo Emerson) to the bridge itself, now guarded by Daniel Chester French's famous minuteman statue.

Daniel Chester French's minuteman statue stands near the North Bridge in Concord.

Beyond the bridge, the land opens onto rolling fields that look virtually unchanged from the 1770s when the Concord militia drilled there. The North Bridge Visitor Center is across the field in the home of Major Buttrick, one of the militia officers. A path to the northwest leads to Colonel Barrett's house, the main munitions depot until the morning of April 19.

Location and Address Minuteman National Historical Park, 174 Liberty Street, Concord, MA 01742. Telephone: (508) 369-6993 or (617) 484-6156.

< 50 >

Operating Hours North Bridge Visitor Center: open daily from 9:00 A.M.–5:30 P.M. Battle Road Visitor Center: open April–November, daily from 8:30 A.M.–5:00 P.M. Wayside Visitor Center: open April to November, daily (except Wednesday) from 9:15 A.M.–9:45 P.M.; December to March, closed Monday.

Entrance fees Wayside Visitor Center: $4.00 for adults; $3.00 per person for groups; admission is free for children under 12. Old Manse: $5.00 for adults; $3.50 for children 6–12.

Exhibits and Events April 19 is the Massachusetts state holiday of Patriots' Day, and the day is commemorated by a number of

Spectators gather to watch a Patriots' Day parade in Concord, Massachusetts.

The North Bridge Commemoration honors the minutemen who fought the redcoats at the battle of Concord.

observances—some on Patriots' Day itself, and others a few days before or after. A week before Patriots' Day, for example, the town of Concord sponsors an afternoon observance called the Meriam's Corner Exercise, which includes a reenactment of the opening shots on Battle Road.

In Concord, Patriots' Day begins with the Dawn Salute at 6:00 A.M., involving hundreds of volunteers dressed in the uniforms and costumes of the period. This is followed by a stirring North Bridge Commemoration at 9:00 A.M., and then a Patriots' Day Parade featuring school bands from many towns in the area.

The historic day is also marked by a ceremony on Lexington Green and a mock battle, with volunteers in uniform displaying the muskets and cannons of the period.

< 52 >

These special ceremonies occasionally change, and the dates and times may also vary. Those interested in the observances and mock battles should check with one of the Visitor Centers of Minuteman National Historical Park, or with the historical society in Lexington (see page 54).

Related Sites

On the road from Concord to Lexington, there are a number of notable stops. These include the Concord Museum (with a visual model of the North Bridge encounter), the Concord Burying Ground (which contains the graves of soldiers who were killed in the fighting), and Wright's Tavern. The tavern was first used as a mustering point for the minutemen, and then, briefly, as a place for British officers to rest. Built in 1747, the building provides an authentic example of the inns and taverns of the period and is now open for tours. Just outside Concord on Route 2A is the Antiquarian Museum. In addition to 15 rooms decorated in historic styles, the museum has one of the Old North Church lanterns.

Another interesting stop is the Lexington Historical Society. One of its exhibits includes the two pistols lost by British Major Pitcairn when his horse bolted to the patriot lines. Also along this road is the Museum of Our National Heritage, which has many Revolutionary War exhibits.

In Lexington, although modern buildings seem to encroach on the past, remarkable reminders of April 19, 1775, can still be seen. At the triangular-shaped Lexington Green, a visitor can stand exactly where the minutemen lined up with Captain Parker. Visitors can stop at the Jonathan Harrington house and Buckman Tavern, where the minutemen gathered. Another stop is the Old Burying Ground, which includes the grave of Captain Parker, as well as those of other

< 53 >

militiamen. Just outside the village center is the Hancock-Clarke House where John Hancock and Samuel Adams were staying when Paul Revere brought the news of the approaching British column. And a mile closer to Boston is Munroe Tavern, which Lord Percy used briefly as his headquarters.

Numerous historic markers are located along Route 2A from Lexington to Charlestown and Boston. Along the route, these markers and several buildings from the Revolutionary War period indicate important events of April 19—such as Lord Percy's placement of his two field cannons and the killing of two of Rachel Cooper's customers by British soldiers at Cooper's Tavern.

A tour through the historic Munroe Tavern gives visitors a look at authentic colonial decor.

Several sites connected to the two historic battles are located in Boston itself. The Old North Church is still intact, although its 190-foot steeple had to be rebuilt after a hurricane in 1954. Nearby is the Paul Revere House National Historic Landmark. It was built in 1670 and is now the oldest wood-frame house in Boston. Guided tours are available daily. Closer to the heart of Old Boston is the "Old Granary" Burial Ground. This quiet little corner in the shadow of modern high-rise buildings contains the graves of John Hancock, Samuel Adams, Paul Revere, and other well-known figures from America's past.

< 54 >

Locations, Addresses, and Operating Hours
Boston

"Old Granary" Burial Ground, corner of Tremont and Bromfield Streets, Boston, MA.

Old North Church National Historic Landmark, 193 Salem Street, Boston, MA 02113. Telephone: (617) 523-6676. Open daily from 9:00 A.M.–5:00 P.M. Admission is free.

Paul Revere House National Historic Landmark, 19-21 North Square, Boston, MA 02113. Telephone: (617) 523-1676. Open from April 15 to October, daily 9:30 A.M.– 5:30 P.M.; November to April 14, Tuesday-Sunday, from 10:00 A.M.– 4:00 P.M. Admission is $2.50 for adults and $1.00 for children 5–17.

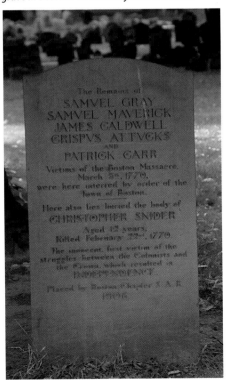

The Boston Massacre victims are buried in this grave in Boston's Old Granary Burial Ground.

Concord and Vicinity

Old Manse National Historic Landmark, Monument Street, P.O. Box 572, Concord, MA 01742. Telephone: (508) 369-3909. Please call for visitor hours as they vary.

Lexington and Vicinity

Museum of Our National Heritage, 33 Marrett Road, Lexington, MA 02173. Telephone: (617) 861-6559. Open Monday–Saturday 10 A.M.–5 P.M., Sunday 12 A.M.–5 P.M. Admission is free.

Lexington Historical Society conducts tours of three Lexington

This mock battle on the Lexington Green is one of the many events held in Lexington on Patriots' Day.

sites from April 19 to October 31. Telephone: (617) 862-1703. Visitor hours are Monday-Saturday 10:00 A.M.–5:00 P.M., Sunday 1:00 P.M.–5:00 P.M. Admission is $4.00 for adults and $2.00 for children. Combination passes for all three sites are also available for $10.00 for adults and $5.00 for children.

Buckman Tavern, Bedford Street, facing the green. Telephone: (617) 862-5598.

Hancock-Clarke House, 35 Hancock Street. Telephone: (617) 861-0928.

Munroe Tavern, 1332 Massachusetts Avenue. Telephone: (617) 674-9238.

CHRONOLOGY OF THE REVOLUTIONARY WAR

September 1774	First Continental Congress meets in Philadelphia.
April 19, 1775	British army and the Massachusetts militia fight at Lexington and Concord near Boston.
May 1775	Massachusetts and Vermont militias capture Fort Ticonderoga on Lake Champlain in New York.
June 1775	Second Continental Congress appoints Washington commander of the Continental Army.
June 1775	Americans fight at the Battle of Bunker Hill.
August 1775– July 1776	American attempts to invade Canada fail.
March 1776	British evacuate Boston for New York.
July 1776	Continental Congress declares the United States independent from Great Britain.
August– November 1776	British under General Howe drive Washington's army out of New York.
December 1776	Washington defeats the British at Trenton, New Jersey.
January 1777	Washington defeats the British at Princeton, New Jersey.
June– October 1777	British General Burgoyne's invasion of New York fails; he surrenders at Saratoga to Horatio Gates.
September– October 1777	Howe defeats Washington at Brandywine and Germantown, Pennsylvania, and occupies Philadelphia.
Winter 1777-78	Continental Army at Valley Forge
February 1778	France and the United States form an alliance.

< 57 >

June 1778	British leave Philadelphia for New York; Washington battles them at Monmouth Courthouse, New Jersey.
July 1778	General Clark captures British posts in the Northwest.
December 1779	British capture Savannah, Georgia.
February–May 1780	British besiege and capture Charleston, South Carolina.
July 1780	4,000 French troops under Rochambeau arrive at Newport, Rhode Island.
August 1780	British under Cornwallis defeat Americans under Gates at Camden, South Carolina.
September 1780	American General Benedict Arnold commits treason and joins the British.
January–March 1781	Nathanael Greene battles Cornwallis in the Carolinas.
January–May 1781	Mutinies occur in the Continental Army.
April 1781	Cornwallis marches from North Carolina to Virginia.
May–August 1781	Cornwallis spars with Lafayette in Virginia and fortifies Yorktown.
August 1781	Washington and Rochambeau march south to join Lafayette and trap Cornwallis at Yorktown.
September–October 1781	Siege of Yorktown
September 1781	French fleet under De Grasse defeats British under Graves in Chesapeake Bay.
October 1781	Cornwallis surrenders at Yorktown.
April 1782	Peace talks begin in Paris between Britain and the United States.
September 1783	Treaty of Paris signed, ending the American Revolution.

FURTHER READING

Bracken, Jeanne M., ed. *The Shot Heard 'Round the World: The Beginnings of the American Revolution*. Carlisle, MA: Discovery Enterprises, 1995.

Brenner, Barbara. *If You Were There in Seventeen Seventy-Six*. Old Tappan, NJ: Simon & Schuster, 1994.

Carter, Alden R. *The American Revolution: War for Independence*. Danbury, CT: Franklin Watts, 1992.

Davis, Burke. *Black Heroes of the American Revolution*. Orlando, FL: Harcourt Brace, 1992.

Forbes, Esther. *America's Paul Revere*. Tarrytown, NY: Marshall Cavendish, 1991.

Fritz, Jean. *Can't You Make Them Behave, King George?* New York: Paperstar, 1996.

Gay, Kathlyn and Martin Gay. *Revolutionary War*. New York: Twenty-First Century Books, 1995.

Johnson, Neil. *Battle of Lexington and Concord*. Old Tappan, NJ: Simon & Schuster, 1992.

King, David C. *America's Story Book 2, Forming a New Nation*. Littleton, MA: Sundance Publishers, 1996.

Melzer, Milton, ed. *The American Revolutionaries: A History in Their Own Words*. New York: Thomas Y. Crowell, 1987.

Murphy, Jim. *A Young Patriot: The American Revolution as Experienced by One Boy*. Boston, MA: Houghton Mifflin, 1995.

Nordstrom, Judy. *Concord and Lexington*. Morristown, NJ: Silver Burdett Press, 1993.

Steins, Richard. *A Nation Is Born: Rebellion and Independence in America*. New York: Twenty-First Century Books, 1993.

WEB SITES

Information about Minuteman National Park can be found at the National Park Service website. This site also includes pictures of some of Minuteman National Park's historic structures. Go to:
http://www.nps.gov/mima

To learn about the history of Lexington, visit the following website:
http://link.ci.lexington.ma.us

To visit the Musuem of Our National Heritage, go to:
http://www.mnh.org

To browse through information about the Revolutionary War, go to:
http://www.uconect.net/~histnact/revwar/revwar.html

To take a virtual tour of the town of Concord, go to:
http://www.concordma.com

SOURCE NOTES

Part One

1. Quoted in David C. King, et al., *United States History* (Menlo Park, CA: Addison-Wesley, 1986), p. 85.

2. Ibid., p. 88.

3. Quoted in Samuel Eliot Morison, *The Oxford History of the American People* (New York: Oxford University Press, 1965), p. 204.

4. Ibid., p. 206.

5. Quoted in Richard B. Morris and the editors of Life, *The Life History of the United States,* vol. 1, *The New World* (New York: Time, Inc., 1963), p. 155.

6. Lord Richmond's speech in Parliament, quoted in Morison, *The Oxford History of the American People*, p. 209.

7. Quoted in Morris, *Life History of the United States,* vol. 1, *The New World*, p. 155.

8. Quoted in Morison, pp. 209–210.

Part Two

1. Allen French, *General Gage's Informers: New Material Upon Lexington and Concord* (Ann Arbor, MI: University of Michigan Press, 1932), pp. 57–58.

2. Quoted in Richard Wheeler, *Voices of 1776: The Story of the American Revolution in the Words of Those Who Were There* (New York: Penguin Books, 1991), p. 3.

3. Ibid., p. 5.

4. Quoted in Richard B. Morris and the editors of Life, *The Life History of the United States,* vol. 2, *The Making of a Nation* (New York: Time, Inc., 1963), p. 8.

5. Reported in the Salem *Gazette*, April 25, 1775, p. 1.

6. Quoted in Milton Melzer, ed., *The American Revolutionaries: A History*

< 61 >

in Their Own Words (New York: Thomas Y. Crowell, 1987), p. 54.

7. Quoted in Wheeler, *Voices of 1776*, pp. 7–8.

8. Quoted in Richard M. Ketchum, et al, eds. *The American Heritage Book of the Revolution* (New York: American Heritage Publishing Co., Inc., 1958), p. 102.

9. Wheeler, *Voices of 1776*, p. 10.

10. Ibid.,p. 11.

11. Quoted in David C. King, *The United States and Its People* (Menlo Park, CA: Adison-Wesley, 1993), p. 96.

12. Ibid., p. 12.

13. Ibid., p. 13.

14. Quoted in David Hackett Fischer, *Paul Revere's Ride* (New York: Oxford University Press, 1994), p. 225.

15. Ibid., p. 231.

16. Ibid.

17. Quoted in Wheeler, *Voices of 1776*, p. 14.

18. Quoted in Fischer, *Paul Revere's Ride*, p. 225.

19. Quoted in Meltzer, *The American Revolutionaries*, pp. 56–57.

20. Rachel Cooper, *The Nineteenth of April, 1775, A Collection of First Hand Accounts*, ed. Clement C. Sawtell (New London, NH: The Country Press, 1968), p. 678.

21. Quoted in Wheeler, *Voices of 1776*, p. 10.

22. Quoted in Fischer, *Paul Revere's Ride*, p. 238.

23. Quoted in Morris, *Life History of the United States,* vol. 2, *The Making of a Nation*, p. 9.

24. Quoted in Wheeler, *Voices of 1776*, p. 19.

25. Patrick Henry, "Give Me Liberty or Give Me Death," *The Annals of America*, vol. 2, *1755–1783, Resistance and Revolution* (Chicago: Encyclopedia Britannica, Inc., 1976), pp. 321–323.

< 62 >

26. Quoted in Fischer, *Paul Revere's Ride*, p. 280.

27. Quoted in Meltzer, *The American Revolutionaries*, p. 59.

28. Ibid.

OTHER SOURCES

American Heritage, editors, *A Guide to America's Greatest Historic Places*. New York: American Heritage, 1985.

Grafton, John, *The American Revolution: A Picture Sourcebook*. New York: Dover, 1975.

Purcell, L. Edward and David Burg, eds., *The World Almanac of the American Revolution*. New York: World Almanac, 1992.

INDEX

< 64 >